DSC SPEED READS

MANAGEMENT

Inductions

John Martin

dsc
directory of social change

Published by the Directory of Social Change (Registered Charity no. 800517 in England and Wales)

Registered address: Directory of Social Change, First Floor, 10 Queen Street Place, London, EC4R 1BE

Tel: 020 4526 5995

Visit www.dsc.org.uk to find out more about our books, subscription funding website and training events. You can also sign up for e-newsletters so that you're always the first to hear about what's new.

The publisher welcomes suggestions and comments that will help to inform and improve future versions of this and all of our titles. Please give us your feedback by emailing publications@dsc.org.uk.

Print and digital editions first published 2024

ISBN 978 1 78482 114 2 (print edition)
ISBN 978 1 78482 115 9 (digital edition)

British Library Cataloguing in Publication Data
A catalogue record for this book is available from the British Library

Cover and text design by Kate Griffith
Printed and bound in the UK by Martins the Printers, Berwick upon Tweed

MIX
Paper | Supporting responsible forestry
FSC™ C013254
FSC www.fsc.org

Contents

Introduction

Who will this book help?

This book is for those who have the responsibility for organising and carrying out inductions for employees and volunteers and for any other staff members involved in the process. It will be of value whether you are a manager, a person responsible for HR, a member of your leadership team or the CEO.

What will it give you?

The success of your organisation depends on your people and how quickly you can get new staff and volunteers up and running happily at full capacity. To achieve this, you need to ensure your new starters understand your organisation and their role within it, and are able to integrate with their new colleagues.

This book shows you how to design a reliable, structured and repeatable induction process that works for both the new starter and for your organisation. It explains what inductions are, why they are important, what makes a good induction, how to plan the process and what types of starter you may need to cater for. There are also tips and pointers that can lift your induction standards from good to excellent.

Chapter 1

Making people welcome

This chapter looks at what inductions are, who they are for, why they are needed and what makes a good induction.

So, you've appointed someone new

Identifying a staffing need... writing the role specification... advertising the offer... shortlisting... interviewing... and making an appointment. Phew, it is easy to believe that you are at the end of the process and can relax. Instead, the most important part of recruitment is about to start. Welcoming and integrating your new member of staff or volunteer into your organisation well is one of the most important management functions you will ever carry out.

What is an induction?

Orientation, onboarding or induction – what are the differences? It is easy to get bogged down in terminology, and there is some debate about the right word to use and what each of them means. Onboarding, for example, could be easily confused with a Winter Olympic sport, whereas induction might bring back memories of learning about magnets in school. Fundamentally, though, all these terms refer to the same process – bringing someone new in and getting them up to speed. It's about hiring people, setting them up on the HR system, training them, showing them around (physically or virtually), involving them in the team, helping them understanding the culture of your organisation and setting goals. Induction is the term commonly used in the UK, and that is what we will be using in this guide.

Who are inductions for?

An induction programme should be carried out for all new starters. This includes volunteers and trustees. You might choose to do a shorter tailored induction for existing staff returning after a period of absence (such as parental leave, extended sick leave or a long sabbatical) or for people changing job roles within the organisation. For simplicity, we refer to all people who would need an induction as new starters in this book. (Google, by the way, calls its new starters Nooglers!)

Why bother?

Every organisation, large or small, should have a well-considered induction programme. It provides the new starter with a positive experience of their organisation, gives them the tools to get started, and helps them to know and become part of the culture of the organisation. It might seem self-evident that well-conducted inductions are a good thing, but the benefits are worth laying out. Well-conducted inductions should:

- Make the new starter feel respected, supported and included. If you get it right and invest time in new people early on, they will reflect that support with commitment to your organisation. Now that remote working is becoming more prevalent, making sure people feel welcomed into your organisation and supported in their role is particularly important.
- Speed up team building. Getting to know a new team early will allow the new starter to understand the dynamics of that team and get used to their role sooner.

- Improve the understanding of your organisational culture. For example, what your charity's equality, equity, diversity and inclusion (EEDI) policies are and what behaviours you endorse as an organisation. It is easier to instil the values and the culture of your workplace from the outset rather than on ad hoc occasions.
- Optimise the new starter's potential and productivity. Not knowing the basics such as how to navigate the IT system, not having the passcode to the photocopier or being unsure whom to contact with an issue can be frustrating and slow the new starter's ability to contribute from day one. Including information on key policies, procedures and seemingly obvious tasks in the induction prevents potential problems.
- Increase employee and volunteer retention. Good inductions help build a solid foundation for new people in an organisation and help their job satisfaction from the very start. Of course, there will be some occasions where the new starter and the organisation are the wrong fit for each other, and a good induction can help identify that. Mostly, though, good inductions should reduce the factors that cause early attrition, such as lack of role clarity and poor integration into the culture.
- Get the best talent. If you treat employees and volunteers well from the outset, your reputation as a good and responsible employer will improve as your people share their experience with friends, family and contacts in other organisations and feed back to recruitment agencies.
- Save money and time. A reliable, structured and repeatable induction process that can be rolled out each time a new starter joins is more efficient than an ad hoc approach. If you have good policies and systems in place, there is no need to completely re-invent the wheel each time. Some of the unchanging and universal elements of the induction can be managed through helpful documentation, good timetabling and effective communication throughout the organisation. This allows you to focus on personalising the induction to the individual and on team building.

The elements of a good induction

The better your induction process, the faster new starters will become confident and comfortable in their roles and be able to fulfil their potential. Your people are usually the most important asset your organisation will have, so showing they are important from the outset will reap its rewards for the productivity and effectiveness of your organisation. You should:

- Establish regular communication channels (whether by letter, email, video-conferencing, telephone or in person) early on. This should include communications between you and the starter, and also between them and other key members of the organisation.
- Make sure there are no surprises. Starting a new role is often a stressful time, so make sure the induction programme is clearly communicated and the new starter knows what to expect.
- Get the paperwork right, including the financial and HR details and key policies that your employees and volunteers need to know from the start.
- Have a structured plan. Your organisation's approach to inductions (see page 9) should ensure reliable standard and repeatable elements for every new starter that works well in most situations.
- Personalise the induction programme where you can. Standard elements in an induction free you to think about what additional bespoke elements will help the individual most.
- Schedule dedicated time for the new starter to read, understand and take in the information you give them. Remember to allocate time for regular breaks in the programme too!
- Not overload them. You don't have to cover everything in a week. Feed in new information gradually and at the appropriate time.

The next chapter gets down to the nuts and bolts of planning the induction and deciding on what the best approach will be for you and the new starter.

Chapter 2

Planning the induction

This chapter looks at styles of induction, the key stages and the induction checklist.

Styles of induction

Most organisations will have some guidance in place to help you plan or manage inductions. This may be a policy, a process or a template. If such standard guidance exists, this should be your starting point. If your organisation does not have a formal policy or established framework for inductions, don't worry. A more tailored induction may be appropriate for the culture and size of your organisation. Also, a hybrid approach – combining some set elements and some flexibility – may suit many organisations. Certainly, standardising parts of the induction for new starters will make the process consistent and ensure you don't miss out crucial elements by mistake. Having an established process in place will be reassuring for the new starter too.

Where next?
Ready-made templates for induction policies can be found online, including one in this bundle from DSC:

www.dsc.org.uk/ppt

Whatever style of induction you choose, it should be suitable to the individual and their needs. Those new to the workplace may require a more formal, directed and specific process to get started; whereas those who have a lot of work experience may benefit from a less-orchestrated approach, where they can control elements of their induction. As long as the process is structured, well-organised, managed and completed in full, it doesn't have to be a rigid affair set out in minute detail.

Advantages of standard and tailored inductions

Standard	Tailored
Consistent – a standard approach may be based on an organisation-wide induction policy that will provide a reliable framework and will ensure that key areas of early information are not missed.	**Adapted** – tailored inductions may suit, for example, an experienced starter, allowing them to shape the induction and tailor it to the needs of their situation, their role and their department.
Planned time – the early days and weeks for the new starter may be set out in detail, which will give certainty at the outset and ensure all areas are covered.	**Flexible time** – activities may change as the induction progresses to focus on areas the new starter finds most useful.
Meeting key colleagues – the standard approach will ensure introductory meetings take place with the CEO, managers, HR personnel and other key individuals.	**Meetings as necessary** – flexibility may mean new starters meet their colleagues when they decide the time is right to do so. For example, this may be when they have had some early information about what their role entails in practice and how they will interact with others (and can make the most of any introductory meetings).
Reliable reading material – key sources of information are readily available and planned into the induction with time to read and understand them.	**Reading material secondary** – may be substituted by a more hands-on approach if that suits the new starter's learning preferences.

The induction process

When does the induction process start? The simple answer is as soon as the candidate accepts the job or volunteering role and certainly before they start. The earlier you engage with your new starter, the more likely they will feel wanted, supported and welcomed warmly into the organisation.

The key stages of the induction process that you will need to think about are outlined in the figure below and explored further in the following subsections.

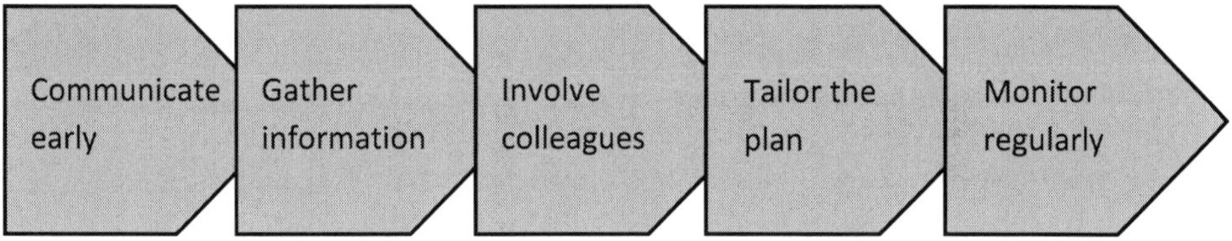

Communicate early

Once the new starter accepts the offer, it is important that you follow up promptly to let them know what happens next. First impressions are crucial, and prompt communication reassures your new starter that you are an efficient and responsible organisation that is really looking forward to them joining the team. Starting a new role is already unsettling, and poor or non-existent communications from your new organisation can make things so much worse.

Gather information

Once the first communications are exchanged, you have some breathing space to think about what further information you need to gather for the induction before the new starter arrives. This might include:

- an organisational chart showing people, roles and how they relate;
- your organisation's vision, mission, objectives and values;
- key policies including induction policy, health and safety information, probation policy (if there is one) and so on;

- finance and HR details;
- summary information about the relevant department or team;
- key internal and external contact lists;
- any publications or resources you think they might find useful;
- sample organisational communications (such as newsletters) to give information on recent activity.

Involve colleagues

Your colleagues will be a key resource in welcoming your new starter and in introducing other departments to them. Make sure you share the details of the new person (including a summary of their previous experience) and that everyone knows their start date. Put in the diary meetings with key individuals well in advance so they are spaced out across the first few days and weeks. Where possible, plan these in order of those who are most important for the starter to meet first. If the new starter's role crosses over with other departments, it may be appropriate for those departments to have an input in the planning of the induction.

Think about arranging a buddy to help look after the new starter. They can be an important link in the induction process, as they provide both a friendly face and an informal source of information. Induction buddies should not have any management responsibility for the new starter, and their role should include all or some of the following:

- Answering questions and providing information. The new starter might be shy to ask what they think are stupid questions – the buddy is there to put them at ease and make them able to raise queries.

- Helping them to find their way around their new workplace – they might be the right person to do the initial tour of the physical office.
- Informally introducing them to colleagues throughout the organisation (in addition to any organised meetings).
- Providing some informal support with aspects of the new starter's role (if the buddy and the new starter are part of the same team).
- Looking after them during breaks in their initial schedule (where they both work from the physical office).
- Immersing them in the culture of the organisation and including them in social activities so that they feel part of the team.

A good induction buddy can be anyone in the organisation who is a good communicator. They may be in a similar role or level of work, and even if they don't work within the same department, they should have some relevant knowledge and experience that will enable them to help the new starter in theirs. The role of a buddy may only be needed for a short time (maybe a month) until the starter has settled in, although in some organisations a longer period may be appropriate.

> **Top tip**
>
> There are some advantages to the buddy not being in the same team – a degree of separation between roles and departments can make the relationship more relaxed.

Tailor the plan

Tailor the induction to the role and individual. If the role is outward-facing and focused on people, such as in fundraising or marketing, meeting people both within and outside the organisation may be a priority. If the job is centred on internal processes, such as accounting or IT, then you may want to concentrate particularly on learning systems quickly. You will want to consider the individual's learning preferences too and offer a variety of ways to take in all the new information – and indeed combine these ways. If they prefer to absorb information through listening, then meeting with colleagues will be important.

If they favour learning through reading or by getting on with tasks, then you might need to allow time for study or hands-on practice. The approach to the induction will also depend on whether the new starter's role is office based or remote. If they are remote, you will need to consider more carefully how they meet their colleagues via video communication platforms, how often you check in with each other and how you share information with them.

Monitor regularly

Make sure you build in and diarise regular review points to see how the induction is going and how the individual is settling in. These can be through formal and regular one-to-ones, but in the early days, an informal catch-up over a cup of coffee or lunch might be appropriate. You will also want to check in with their immediate colleagues and, if you have a buddying system (see page 12), with their buddy to get a sense how the new starter is adjusting to their new environment.

New starter induction checklist

A useful feature of your induction guidance will be a standard checklist, which will help your planning, make sure you do things in the right order and ensure you don't miss out anything important (see chapter 3 for more on the various tasks mentioned in the induction checklist). Use it as a guide but add things that are specific to the new starter or to the needs of the department. Share it with the individual when they start so that they know what will happen during their induction. They will be able to tick tasks off as they are completed. This gives them a sense of control and ownership over their induction process; however, ultimately, the line manager should be responsible for seeing that the list is completed and signed off. You can add notes too – either in advance or as you complete items. It is helpful to allocate responsibility for the activities to ensure everyone knows who is doing what and everything is completed.

Sample new starter induction checklist

Action	Notes	Responsibility	Date complete
Confirmation letter, introductory pack and welcome	Include role description, invite to office social (before start date) and welcome card from all staff	Sam Smith, HR Officer	
Welcome email from CEO	CEO to welcome new starter at all-staff meeting	Jan Jones, CEO	
Meet HR to complete essential admin (sign contracts, fill in payroll forms, receive their P45 form, go over key health and safety points, fire regulations and annual leave allowance, confirm emergency contacts, etc.)	If signed contract not received already, ensure it is with HR	Sam Smith, HR Officer	
Office orientation including toilets, fire escapes, kitchen and water coolers		Ali Alvarez, Line Manager	
Briefly introduce key colleagues	Ensure fuller meetings are in the diary with colleagues	Ali Alvarez, Line Manager	
Introduce work station		Ali Alvarez, Line Manager	

Key details to get started, such as email login, telephone number, Zoom password and so on		Alex Adams, IT Manager	
Immediate training needs, for example email and server structure (note future training, such as database training)		Ali Alvarez, Line Manager	
Recurring diary dates, such as team lunch, check-ins and key meetings		Ali Alvarez, Line Manager	
Key policies (e.g. sickness, probationary period, disciplinary practice, annual leave and dress code)		Ali Alvarez, Line Manager	
Buddy to feed back to line manager on progress		Kit Kramer, Buddy	
Add in…	Following early meetings between the line manager and new starter, additional activities might be identified and agreed	Jamie Jessop, new starter	
Add in…	Additional activities to be agreed in the first week	Jamie Jessop, new starter	

Chapter 3

Early days

This chapter looks at details of getting ready for your new starter, their first day, first week and beyond.

Before the start date

There is a lot you can do to prepare for your new starter before they arrive, so get all your ducks in a row well before they start.

Early communication and paperwork

> **Where next?**
> For detailed HR and employment information go to:
>
> *www.gov.uk/browse/employing-people/recruiting-hiring*
>
> *www.acas.org.uk*

There can sometimes be a yawning gap between the interview and starting date, so keep the new starter engaged and ensure they get all the key documents they need before they start. Your first written communication with your new starter may come from their line manager or from the person responsible for HR, depending on the size of your organisation. As with all first impressions, it gives the starter an immediate sense of what your organisation is like. It should be a welcome message confirming the role offer and may include a request for references if not already obtained. The communication should confirm the job title, together with role specifications and responsibilities, the agreed salary for staff, the starting date and arrival (if you have an office) or starting (if remote working) instructions. It will include details of any paperwork required in advance or that the new starter should bring with them on the first day. For staff, this includes their P45 from previous employment or, if not available or known, their national insurance number, date of birth, address, passport, next of kin details, what kind of student loan they may have and so on. Much of this information will be needed for HR purposes or for your finance team to fill in for HMRC.

The initial communication should establish whether any reasonable adjustments may be needed to enable the new starter to carry out their role and whether an early discussion with the person responsible for HR would be required (see www.acas.org.uk/reasonable-adjustments). You can include other details in an extended Welcome Pack or, to avoid overloading the new starter, let them know that additional information will follow later or be available on the first day of work. These further elements may include:

- staff or volunteer handbook;
- key contact details;
- schedule for the first day at work or the full induction plan if ready;
- your induction policy.

It is a good idea to follow up the initial written communication with a call to talk through what the new starter might expect on the first day and to answer any initial queries.

Workspace

Consider where the new starter will sit within the team and how it relates to their work. If their role requires concentration on a specific task for extended periods, they may need a separate office or a quieter position in an open-plan area and/or may need headphones. If the role requires regular team interaction, then an open-plan area would be right for them. If they are in a quieter, separate area for their role, think about how you can actively integrate them into the team, for example through regular team meetings, group coffee mornings or other social events.

Where the role is remote or mostly remote, consider whether the new starter needs to set aside periods of time in their day with no meetings or to have a 'do not disturb' notification on. If they need to work more closely with their colleagues, or prefer to be with others, you might explore the option of virtual offices – where people can work together on an online or video communication platform similarly to sharing a physical office space. A shared physical co-working hub might also work for certain meetings or as a regular change of scenery.

Whether the workspace is in a physical office or the new starter will be working remotely, make sure that everything they will need is in place in good time and certainly on the start date. Try to avoid kitting out the new starter with the half-chewed pens of other staff and the laptop that had drinks spilled on it at the work party. A clean and neatly presented set-up will give a good initial impression of your organisation.

Don't forget about the health and safety risk assessment (which can be a self-assessment) of the working environment for all employees – whether working at the office or from home – which is a legislative requirement of The Management of Health and Safety at Work Regulations 1999.

Where next?

Useful advice on health and safety risk assessments can be found at:

www.hse.gov.uk/simple-health-safety/risk/index.htm

Some new starters may have specific workplace needs regarding a disability or health condition, so this is an important question to ask when they agree to the role offer. For remote workers, you will need to arrange for any equipment to be sent to them and to check they have a suitable room to work in and appropriate furniture. You may also need to clarify what policies you have for working from home and what contribution the organisation makes for any equipment and/or adjustments (this could include whether there is an allowance for increased telephone and broadband use, heating and lighting).

IT

Ensure the new starter has an identity and is set up on your systems. They should have a telephone number (if they have a telephone), an email address and relevant security passes to be able to access all necessary areas of your organisation's server, including any internal intranets, shared drives or messaging systems, before they start. For some organisations, security of information and data may be particularly important, especially if you have people working remotely. Make sure the new starter knows what your policies and expectations are.

The first day

On day one, the focus should be on essential tasks and information only. This includes an overall sense of the ethos, culture, values and ambition of the organisation. Get them enthused!

Greeting on arrival

Decide who would be the best person to greet the new starter when they arrive. Usually, it would be their line manager, but it might be the person responsible for HR, with whom they may have already had some contact at the interview stages. If you have more than one person starting at the same time for different departments, it might make sense for the person responsible for HR to greet and meet them together. If the new starter is a remote worker and their first day is online, you will need to arrange an equivalent online meeting to ensure a proper welcome.

> **Top tip**
> It is a nice touch to ensure there is a welcome email or card from your CEO waiting for the new starter.

Getting the red tape out of the way

As well as offering a warm and informal welcome, you should use the first day to sort out any outstanding paperwork. Just as with the initial greeting, the person responsible for HR or line manager will often lead this formal meeting. It's a chance to sign the contract (if it hasn't been signed already) and to brief essential policies such as health and safety and fire regulations.

Tour of the workplace

The person responsible for HR, line manager or buddy (see page 12) may carry out the initial tour of the workplace (assuming your organisations has an office). It is good practice to do this. It allows the new starter to orientate themselves, get a sense of where departments are and, most importantly, be able to find facilities like the toilets and washing areas, the kitchen (if you have one) and drinking water. For health and safety purposes, you should point out the first aid facilities and identify the fire exits.

For remote workers or for organisations that are completely virtual, the tour will be different, but it is still important. You might choose to introduce the new starter to areas of your server, the intranet or the internal communications platform for your organisation. You may also use the opportunity to discuss their working space at home to ensure it is suitable for work purposes (see page 18).

Breaks

There will be a lot of information to absorb for the new starter, so ensure there are breaks for them to take a breath. The buddy should be available to take them for a coffee. While breaks are essential, make sure there aren't big gaps in the day where the new starter is aimless and doesn't know what to do.

The first week, first month and beyond

The first day has been completed successfully. Your new starter has been welcomed, had a broad introduction to where they will be working, been given a small amount of information and met some key people. You and the new starter can now look further ahead to the first week and months to come.

Meeting colleagues

While you will not want to overload the new starter with too many new faces, it is good to plan regular but well-spaced meetings in the diary over the first few weeks so they can familiarise themselves with other people in the organisation. Get the meetings in their diary and agree with colleagues what the meetings will cover. People to meet could include:

- senior managers – the heads of the main departments or teams in the organisation;
- team members – the people they are going to work most closely with;
- CEO – if appropriate to the size of your organisation, meeting the CEO will help with giving the new starter the wider picture;
- other departments – teams the new starter might work with often.

The main purpose of initial meetings with colleagues is to ensure a friendly and inspiring welcome. It can be useful for each department to prepare a short briefing sheet to share in advance of the meeting, so the starter can think of questions to ask and to focus the meeting. The sheet should include a brief description of their overall purpose and activities, as well as the individual roles and team set-up (if possible, include staff photos). It helps to populate the briefing with some data to give context and, importantly, to make it more relevant by describing where and when the new starter might come into contact with the department. For instance, in the example overleaf, the fundraising team representatives are meeting a new starter in the press office, and you can see from the brief bullets how the two teams interact. First days can be a blur, so having some information for the new starter to look over before and after each of the meetings can be useful.

Fundraising department – induction notes for new starters

Fundraising team

Ali Alvarez – Head of Fundraising (4 days per week, not Friday)

Ali is responsible for:

- Fundraising strategy
- Budgeting and monthly income/expenditure reporting
- Major donor fundraising and key accounts

Jerry Jones – Trust Fundraiser (full time)

Jerry is responsible for:

- Trust fundraising
- Management of volunteers
- Some corporate fundraising

Background to the fundraising department

ABC Charity has been fundraising since the charity was formed in the 1990s to support people with X syndrome. We started with one volunteer fundraiser and now have a small team of two paid staff and occasional volunteers. Our aim is to double our fundraising by 2030 and we plan to add a corporate fundraiser to our team in 2026. In our current campaign, we have been highlighting the stories of the families and carers of people with X syndrome. The campaign has been particularly targeted at leisure magazines through articles and adverts, and so we have worked closely with the press office.

Fundraising income

Year	Trust fundraising	Major donor fundraising	Other fundraising	Overall income
2022	£45,000	£95,000	£10,000	£150,000
2023	£50,000	£105,000	£15,000	£170,000
2024	£65,000 budget	£115,000 budget	£15,000 budget	£195,000 budget

Interaction with the press office

We work closely with the press office, particularly with regards to our fundraising campaigns, including on:

- Press releases on fundraising campaigns and achievements
- Photo opportunities
- Press enquiries about our cause

First tasks

It is possible that the previous employee or volunteer has left some tasks to be done straight away. Where that is the case, let the new starter know that the induction might need to be spread over a longer period. If they need to hit the ground running, introduce the urgent tasks as needed; however, ideally, start feeding tasks to them gradually and no earlier than day two.

Information and training

Continue to provide information to the new starter as required, building it up steadily. If you have a staff newsletter or communication that goes out to members or beneficiaries, get the new starter on the mailing list. Ensure they have plenty of time allocated to become familiar with IT and communication systems and any technical aspects of the role.

Regular one-to-ones

Get regular one-to-ones in place as a routine – initially at least weekly and then stretched to fortnightly or monthly, depending on specific circumstances. In the early weeks, the induction should be reviewed regularly as part of the one-to-ones. Give the starter opportunities to ask questions and to discuss any concerns they have.

Performance review

By the end of six months or the end of the probation period, if there is one as part of the starter's contract, a formal performance review should be carried out to assess progress, longer-term training needs and future targets. Reviewing how effective the induction has been may form part of this meeting or be carried out separately.

If the new starter is not performing as expected, you may need to identify further support if required. They may need extra supervision or training, or more regular one-to-ones and feedback to ensure they are on track for their targets. Make sure that any performance issues are raised as soon as possible rather than waiting for the performance review. Of course, do give people time to make mistakes and learn; however, if there are serious and genuine concerns, deal with them promptly. They shouldn't come as a surprise at the performance review. If the outcome of the performance review is that dismissal is necessary, that should be carried out in line with your disciplinary and dismissal procedures, with the correct notice period and remuneration.

Case study

'Before I officially started at DSC, I was designated a buddy from the research team, whose job was to help me settle in remotely. My buddy provided me with a staff list and an induction plan they had created for me. My line manager and the HR officer also got in touch to make final arrangements. This prepared me for my first day.

'On my first day, I was welcomed at our daily check-in, where I briefly and virtually met my colleagues. Throughout the days that followed, I met each department individually. During these meetings, each department gave me an overview of their responsibilities, and we discussed how my role linked with theirs, allowing me to build a picture of how DSC's cogs turn.

'The whole office also threw me an online welcome party, and the research team sent me a welcome card! It takes time to adjust to a new role, especially when starting a job remotely, so all these friendly gestures made me feel very welcome and supported.'

Kalli Jayasuriya, Researcher, DSC

Chapter 4

Types of starter

This chapter looks at different types of new starter.

The purpose of inductions is the same for all new starters – to help people become an effective part of your organisation. But for particular types of starter, such as those returning to work after illness or those entering workforce for the first time, you may need to adjust your standard approach to suit those particular circumstances.

New career starters

If your new starter is coming to you straight from completing their education or initiating a career later in their life, their new role may be their first formal employment and it may be their first induction. They may be nervous and less certain about what is expected, how to behave and where they fit into your organisation than people who have been around the block a few times. You may need to place more emphasis on briefing them on core information, supporting them with one-to-ones and having a buddy on hand.

A recruit or transferring employee may be changing roles because they wish to apply recent learning they have completed, or because the job they are moving to accommodates or complements a new course or qualification they are undertaking. Induction needs will vary, but the induction should be flexible and take advantage of any new skills and knowledge.

Return to work and change of role

Your new starter may be experienced but returning to your organisation after a break or a change of circumstances. These situations might include:

- **Sabbatical:** These might occur where the individual needs extra time for family commitments, for a volunteering role, to develop new skills or simply an extended holiday. They may return to the same job or a different role with your organisation. The induction will need to be adjusted to the length of the break and take into account the nature of leave.
- **Childcare and other caring responsibilities:** It is possible your new starter might have caring responsibilities for their family and that their new role needs to fit around external responsibilities. The induction will need to reflect and take account of their situation by, for example, being done partially by online meetings.
- **Maternity, adoption or shared parental leave:** Where the person is starting work a year after their child's birth or being matched for adoption, a lot will have gone on in their lives since they were last at work. It may be that the individual will need to come back to an adapted role or work different hours. They may not be up to date and remember all aspects of their role.
- **A long-term illness:** Consider whether reasonable adjustments to their work environment might be needed as a result of health needs and factor that into your induction checklist. They may not be returning to exactly the same role as before and may return in a phased way or to a different work pattern, such as a job share (where responsibilities for a role are divided between two or more people) or part-time hours.
- **Interim role:** The type of induction will depend on the amount of time the person has been away and the nature of the work they have been performing. They may feel like they have taken a back step by returning to a previous role and feel dispirited or embarrassed, so your job will be to help them feel comfortable and engaged again, for example through emphasising the value of their role through your induction meetings.

- **Redundancy:** An individual may be taking up a new role after being made redundant from their previous job. They are likely to bring valuable skills and experience – make sure your induction process makes the most of that and ensure the new starter feels engaged and motivated in their new role.
- **Relocation:** The person may be starting in their new role because they have moved to a different area where they could not continue in their previous job or volunteering role, or they may be returning from time abroad. Such people may need more time or help with orientating in their new location or more social support to make them feel welcome.

In all situations, the new starter may have become rusty with regards to certain aspects of their role, especially if their specialism is a fast-moving area, or they may have forgotten certain tasks and so need a refresher. Colleagues may have changed since their absence and so meeting unfamiliar faces would form part of the return-to-work induction.

Remote workers

Increasingly, work is not limited to office space, and many organisations do not have offices at all but meet up either partially or entirely in the virtual sphere. With remote workers, particular consideration should be given to equipment and their working environment to ensure that both are suitable and appropriate (see also page 18). You may also need to go the extra mile to embed the new starter in the social aspects of your organisation, which is often easier to do in a physical workplace because of the face-to-face proximity. The role of the buddy may be particularly important here to help introduce the new starter more informally to the rest of the organisation. More regular check-ins will also help to ensure they are settling in well. You might want to highlight to the new staff member or volunteer the informal communication opportunities open to them, for example a fantasy football group, a book club on the intranet or a well-being channel on your internal communications platform.

Volunteers and trustees

> **Where next?**
> Useful information on board inductions:
>
> *www.gettingonboard.org/free-guides-for-charities*

Volunteers should expect to receive inductions to the same level as employees, relevant to the tasks they are carrying out and proportionate to the time they are giving to your organisation. Indeed, most of the information covered in this guide applies to volunteers as much as it does for staff. While the arrangement for volunteers may be less formal than for employees, it is important they know their role and what is expected of them, whom they are responsible to and where to go to with questions or problems. Make sure they receive a tour of the workplace, are introduced to key staff, familiarise themselves with any important information, including key policies such as health and safety, and have training relevant to their role. They should know how to claim necessary expenses related to their volunteering and when they can take breaks. Volunteers often give their time around other responsibilities such as childcare, and you should make an effort to accommodate their needs.

It is important that new trustees (who are also volunteers) are up to speed quickly, because they have a decision-making role within your organisation. They will benefit from seeing documents such the charity's governing document, the board's role and responsibilities, the code of governance, any strategy documents, recent minutes and the most recent annual report and accounts. New trustees should meet the chair of the board, other trustees, the CEO and key members of the leadership team early on.

> **Top tip**
> It is a nice thought to present your new trustees with a resource such as *The Charity Trustee's Handbook* or *It's a Battle on the Board.*
>
> *What Have Charities Ever Done For Us*? is a great introduction to the sector for all staff and volunteers.

Internships and job shadowing

You may have people who have a short-term presence in your organisation – perhaps on work experience, a more formal internship or in a shadow role to learn from a specific member of your organisation. They may require a shorter version of the induction, depending on why they are with you and how long they are staying.

In these short-term situations you may choose to, for example, not introduce them formally to the whole organisation but just to the department where they will be based. Apart from essential health and safety requirements, you may not need to walk them through all of the formal paperwork either.

Not quite the induction the new starter was expecting.

Chapter 5

Inspirational inductions

This chapter looks at how small changes can move your inductions from the humdrum to inspirational.

Making it personal

Knowing something about your new starter can help break the ice and integrate them into your organisation more seamlessly. Perhaps you noticed on their CV that they are a keen follower or participant in sports. If you have a sweepstake for a sporting event that they have an interest in, why not ask the organiser to contact them in their first week to see if they want to participate. If work colleagues get together for a social event – a trip to cinema, for example – invite them along as it will make it easier to help them feel part of the team sooner.

Away days

If your organisation is holding an away day before the new starter officially joins, invite them along without the expectation that they must attend. Make it clear that they won't be on show or expected to participate as fully as others, but with the aim of meeting colleagues and starting to get a feel of the organisation's culture.

Groups and forums

Get new starters involved early in any voluntary groups. It could be a well-being group, staff forum or cross-departmental project. All of these are a good way for the new starter to meet people from other departments and get an insight into what makes your organisation tick.

A cycle of improvement

Who's better to say if your inductions are as good as they can be than those going through the induction? Ask for honest feedback on the process from the people who have recently joined your organisation. They will be perfectly placed to highlight what might be missing or could have been done better. In fact, why not try to involve them in the next induction as, say, a buddy?

A final note

The importance of excellent inductions cannot be over-emphasised. If you want engaged, enthusiastic and well-equipped people who will quickly become productive for your organisation, then inductions are one of the strongest tools you have. To that end, this case study that closes the book really hits the mark.

Case study

Jill Thornton, a canny HR Officer in the charitable sector, had a lightbulb moment in her organisation. She had noticed how much care, effort and attention the organisation was spending on people that were leaving – farewell cards, gifts, exit interviews and parties abounded. She realised that it was, to put no finer words on it, all slightly arse about face.

While the organisation wished leavers well and everyone was very sad to see them move on to pastures new, it was the new starters they had a bigger responsibility towards and that was where the investment of time and effort would be best focused. That realisation led to the introduction of a welcome card and party for all new starters. Starting well made it easier to finish well too because the leavers' experience of the organisation was usually very positive from induction to exit.